Tips

- Keep your child's supplies in a container so that everything is close at hand.
- Explain directions before your child begins a new type of activity.
- Show your child how the illustrations help show what to do.
- Encourage your child to pick up and throw away all scraps when a project is finished.

Supplies

- scissors
- glue stick or paste
- crayons or colored pencils
- marking pens
- pencil
- clear tape
- some projects may require additional supplies

Table of Contents

Funny Monkey

Practice drawing a monkey.

Miss Monkey

Fill in the boxes.

Word Box

banana bow feet neck smile

What is the mystery word? ____________

Monkey, Monkey, MOO

Monkey Chain

1. Cut out the monkeys on pages 7 and 9.
2. Hang the monkeys to make a chain.
   Put the monkeys in this order:

   brown
   green
   yellow
   purple
   red
   blue
3. Read the poem on the back of the monkeys.

Monkey, Monkey, moo
Can you name a few?
Yellow monkeys,
Purple monkeys,
Monkeys red
and blue.

1

Monkey, Monkey, moo

2

Can you name a few?

3

Yellow monkeys,

4 Purple monkeys,

5 monkeys red

6 and blue.

Hungry little monkey went up
a banana tree.
When she reached the top,
how many did she see?

Favorite Food

Pretend you are the monkey.
Color the bananas yellow.

How many bananas can you find?

Fish, Fish, Fish

1, 2, 3, 4, 5
I caught a fish alive.
6, 7, 8, 9, 10
I let it go again.

Why did you let it go?
Because it bit my finger so.
Which finger did it bite?
The little one on the right.

Connect the dots.

Swim, Fish, Swim

1. Cut out the six sections of the fish.
2. Beginning at number one, insert a fastener through the top of the white dot into the left side of section two.
3. Continue until all six pieces are assembled.
4. Then, swim little fish, swim!

Fish Twins

Circle the two fish that are the same.

Origami in the Fishbowl

1. Pull out page 17. Cut out the shapes.
2. Fold the paper shapes to make two fish.
3. Glue the tail on each fish.
4. Glue the sea grass, the little house, and the fish in the fishbowl on page 19.

fold
fold
fold
fold
fold
fold

In the Fishbowl

Underwater Surprise

Color the fish.

What Is Happening?

Something is going on.
What do you think is happening?

A Long Way from Home

Draw a line from the fish to the castle.

Dogs

Dogs come in all sizes and shapes.
Can you guess our names?

Sandy is bigger than Peppy.
Peppy is the last dog.
Annie is between Sandy and Angus.
Angus has spots.

Waldo's Dog

Hop along as you say the poem.

Waldo's dog is a
1-legged dog,
1-legged dog,
1-legged dog.

Waldo's dog is a
2-legged dog,
2-legged dog,
2-legged dog.

Waldo's dog is a
3-legged dog,
3-legged dog,
3-legged dog.

Waldo's dog is a
4-legged dog,
4-legged dog,
4-legged dog.

Dog Stuff

FIDO

Make a ring around the words you can find.

Word Box

ears	tongue	tail
collar	fur	paws

p	a	w	s	c	s	d	t
d	o	g	z	o	r	o	o
e	d	o	f	l	t	g	n
a	c	a	t	l	a	b	g
r	r	u	n	a	i	a	u
s	f	u	r	r	l	l	e
s	e	e	d	o	g	l	m

How many times did you find the word dog in the puzzle?

Friendly Fido

Draw to match.

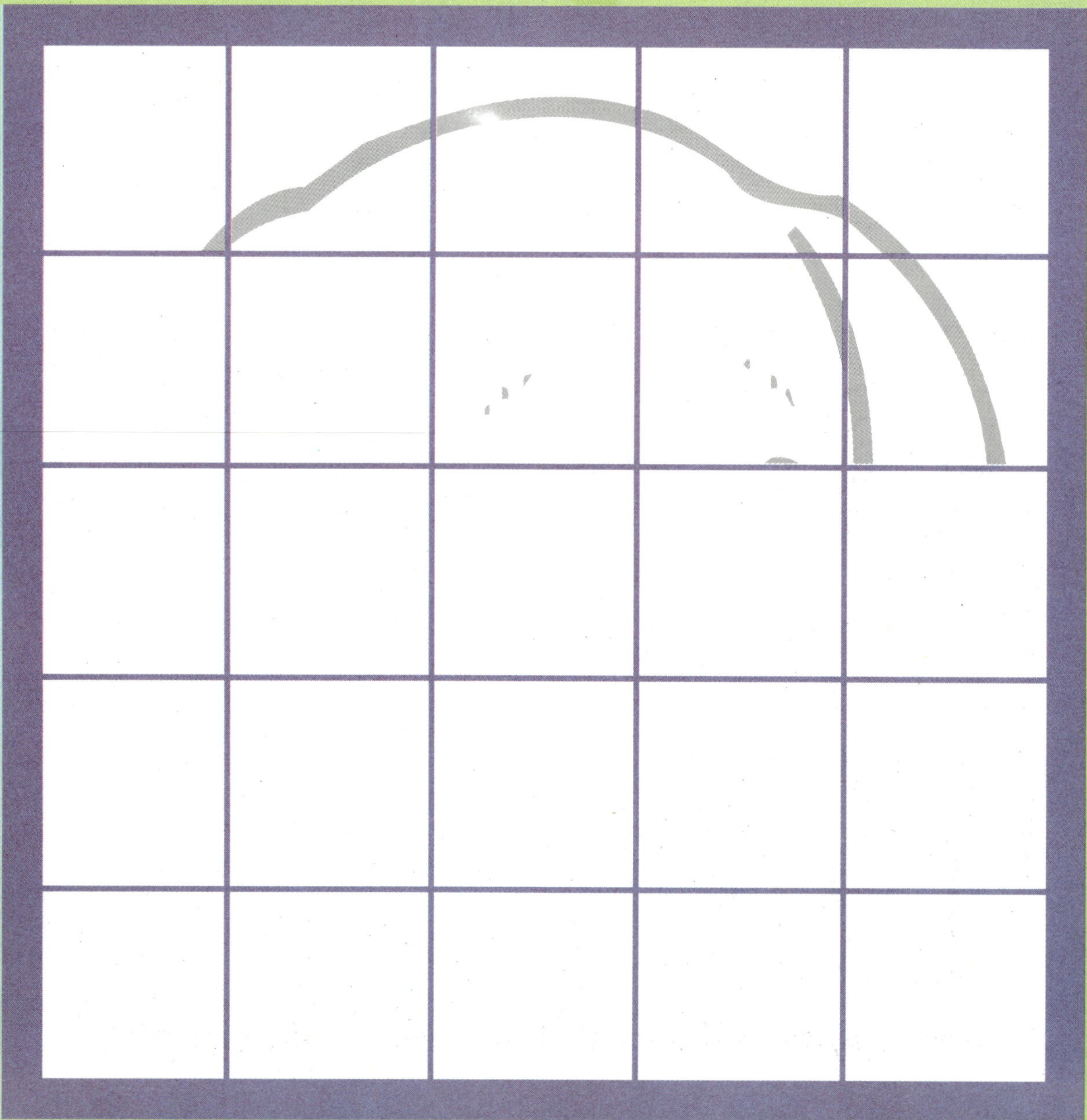

My Dog

My dog has a long tail,
pointed ears, black spots,
and brown eyes.
Can you find him?

Circle my dog.

Bow Wow

Connect the dots.

Dog Bones

Find the bones for the hungry puppy. Color them.

Paper Tube Dog

1. Cut out the dog parts.
2. Fold on the lines.
3. Glue the patterns to the tube.

fold
fold
front
back

My Paper Tube Dog

Wag, beg, bark, and lick.
Run, dig, fetch a stick.
That's my dog!

My dog's name is_________________________.

My dog likes to _________________________.

My dog and I go _________________________.

My dog does funny tricks.______________

____

Set your paper tube dog here.

Clowning Around

Act as a clown as you read the poem.
Then color the clowns and balloons.

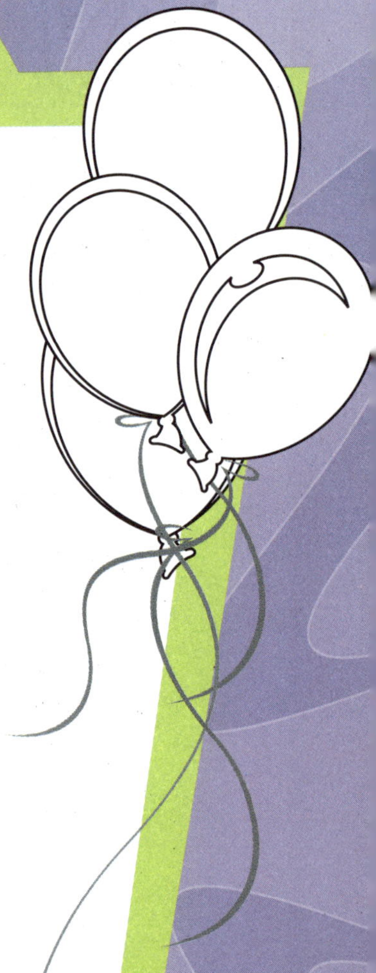

Little clown, little clown,
Turn around.

Little clown, little clown,
Jump up and down.

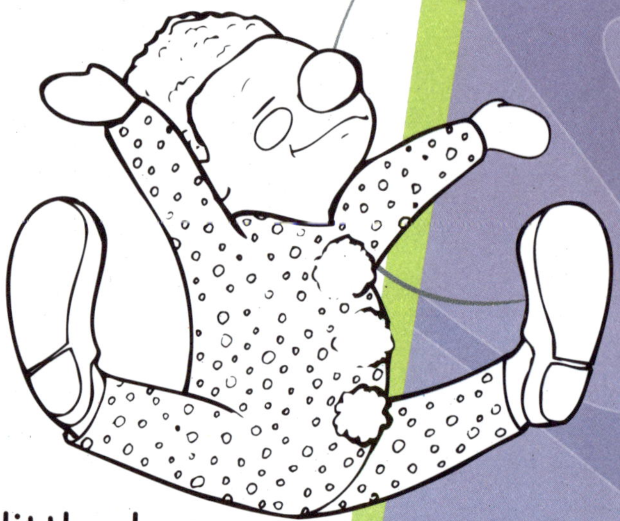

Little clown, little clown,
Touch your shoe.

Little clown, little clown,
That will do.

Which 2 Are Alike?

Circle the two clowns that are the same.

Clown Tricks

Cut out the clown parts on page 37.
Glue them below.

Clown Tricks

Clown Mask

Cut out the mask.
Punch holes as marked.
Add a string to each side.
Tie it around your head.
Make someone laugh.

Funny Clown

Draw and color the other side of the clown.

Leo, the Looooong Dog

1. Cut out the dog parts.
2. Fold the middle part.
3. Glue the parts together.

glue
fold
fold
fold
glue

Word Search

Find the words from the word box in the word search.

c l o w n d m f

t r i c k o c u

s m i l e g l n

h t e n t c o n

a r i d e a w y

t n o s e r n z

u p c i r c u s

s c l o w n r t

Word Box

car clown funny smile trick

circus dog hat tent

How many times did you find the word clown?

Fun with Insects

Let's catch some insects.

1. Cut out the Insect Catcher on page 47.
2. Do the word search. Try to find the words you see in the Word Box.
3. Fold on the lines.
4. Cut out the insects on page 49.
5. Put them in the Insect Catcher and close the flaps. Show them to a friend.

Insect Catcher

Circle the insects in the puzzle.

w	b	u	t	t	e	r	f	l	y
a	a	s	k	m	o	t	h	e	f
s	n	b	e	e	t	l	e	s	l
p	t	l	a	d	y	b	u	g	y
b	o	w	b	o	g	d	o	g	t
u	h	o	n	e	y	b	e	e	n
g	l	r	n	k	b	u	g	o	z

How many times did you find bug? ◯

Word Box

beetle
bug
butterfly
fly
honeybee
ladybug
moth
wasp

Insect Catcher
Name:

ladybug

dragonfly

ant

butterfly

honeybee

fly

wasp

moth

beetle

Look Carefully

Circle the two ladybugs that are the same.

Lovely Ladybugs

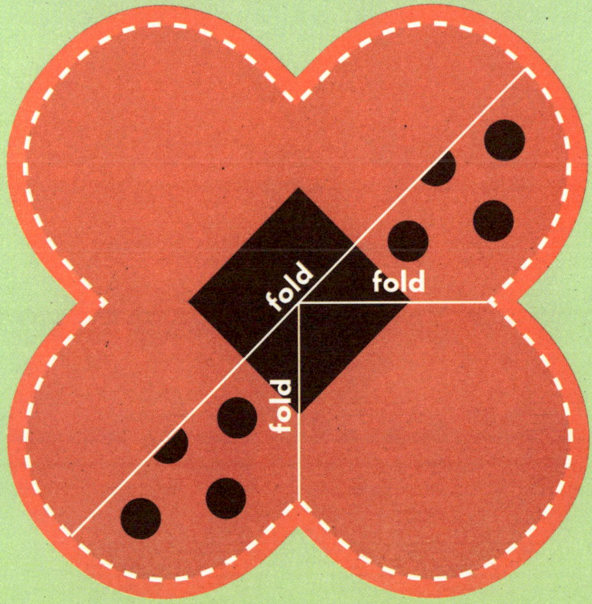

1. Cut out the patterns.
2. Fold on the lines.
3. Glue the ladybugs on the leaves on page 52.

Anyone Home?

Help the ant find his friend.

Pretty Butterfly

A butterfly is an insect, too.
Draw and color the other side of the butterfly.

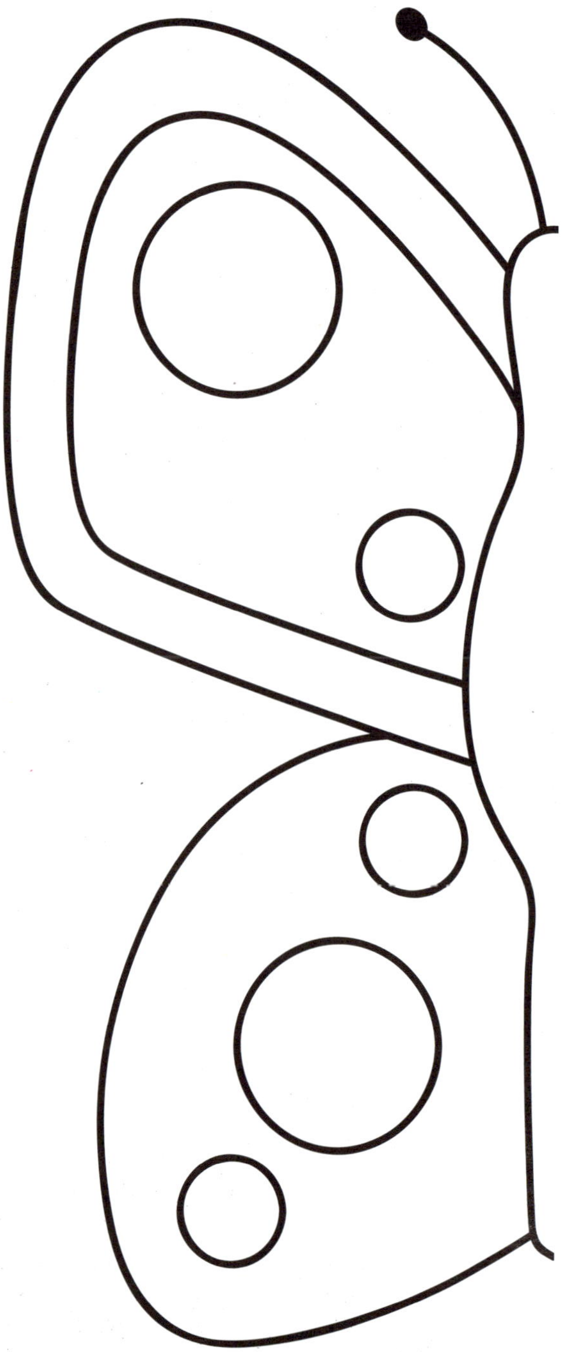

Honeybee Hunt

Honeybees are insects, too.
How many honeybees can you find?
Color them.

Mix and Match Dragonflies

Cut out the wings and glue them onto the dragonfly bodies on page 58.

A Bunch of Bears

Try acting out this rhyme while jumping rope with your friends.

Teddy Bear

Teddy Bear, Teddy Bear,
Turn around.
Teddy Bear, Teddy Bear,
Touch the ground.

Teddy Bear, Teddy Bear,
Go upstairs.
Teddy Bear, Teddy Bear,
Say your prayers.

Teddy Bear, Teddy Bear,
Turn out the light.
Teddy Bear, Teddy Bear,
Say "Good night."

My Bear Puppet

You will need a small paper bag, scissors, and glue.

1. Cut out the pattern pieces on page 63.
2. Glue them to the bag as shown.
3. Put your hand in the bag. Let the bear puppet tell your favorite bear story.

Bear sleeps through the winter
Then awakes in the spring.

Bear wakes up so hungry
He'll eat most anything.

Bear Parts

Circle the words you find.

c	e	a	r	s	x	c	n
g	m	b	e	a	r	l	o
o	o	t	a	i	l	a	s
b	u	a	n	p	a	w	e
e	t	b	e	a	r	s	e
e	h	t	b	e	a	r	y
s	n	o	u	t	o	n	e

How many times did you find bear in the puzzle? ◯

Word Box

paw	tail	eye
snout	mouth	nose
ears	claws	bear

The Three Bears

A Pop-Up Book

1. Cut out the patterns.
2. Make the pop-up book.
3. Glue the bears to the tabs.
4. Open and close the holder as you tell the story of The Three Bears and that naughty little Goldilocks.

cut
fold
cut
cut
fold
cut

The Three Bears

A Hungry Bear

Count by 2s to connect the dots.

Draw Bears

Practice drawing a bear.

Now make your bear dance and play.

Elephants

Trace the path to the water hole.

I'm Hungry

Help the elephant find a snack.

Elephants on Parade

1. Cut out the elephants on the black dotted lines on page 75.
2. Fold the elephant in half.
3. Cut out the ears.
   Glue the ears to the body.
4. Cut on the trunk line. Fold it up and glue it together.
5. Cut the tail. Bend it.
   Fold up the feet.

Place your elephants on the table.
You have a parade of elephants.

fold
fold
fold
fold
fold
fold

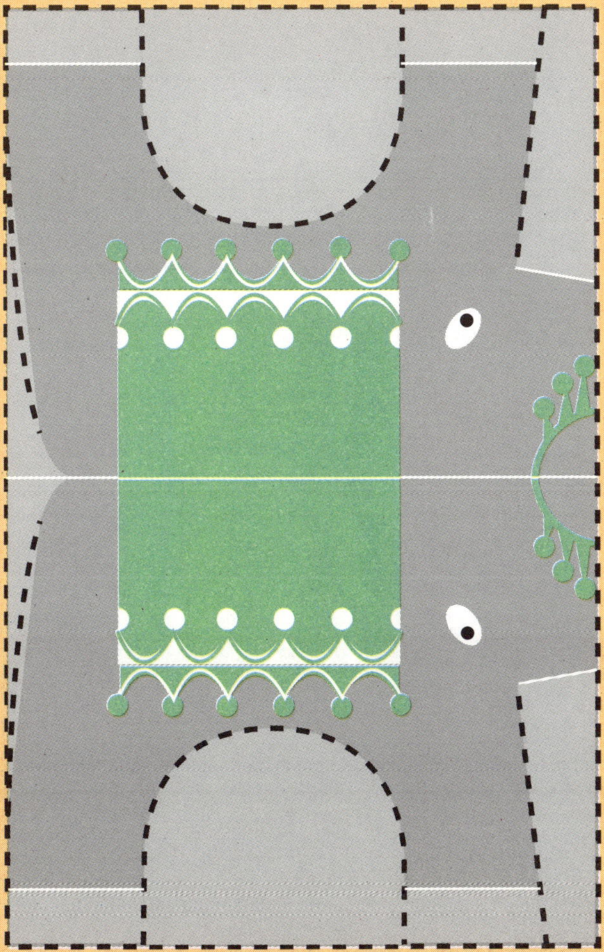

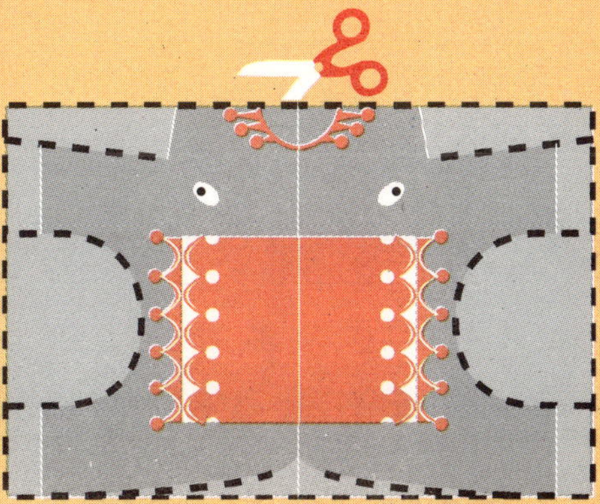

Draw to Match

Draw the elephant on the grid.

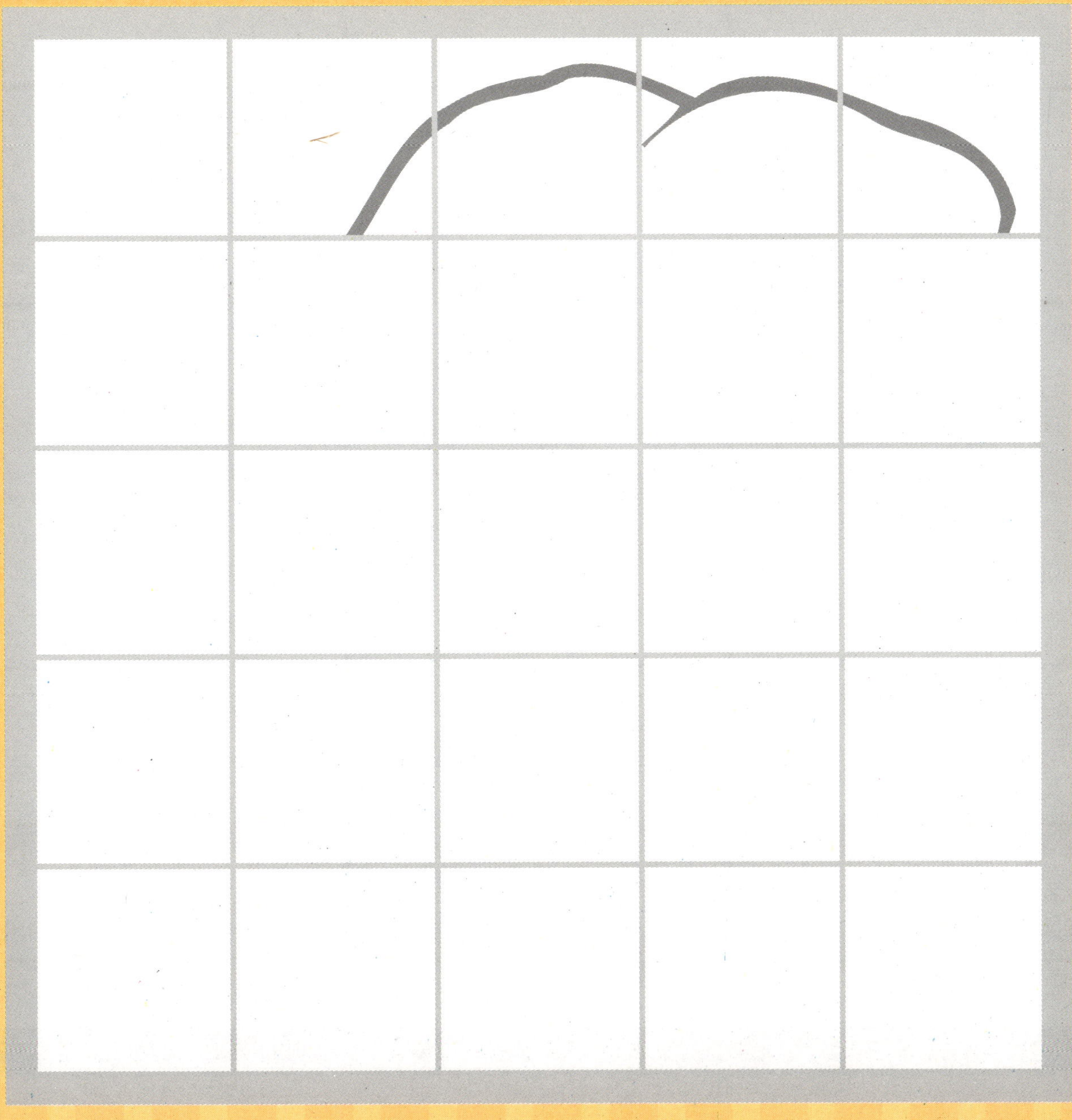

Under the Big Top

glue	glue	glue
glue	glue	glue
glue	glue	glue
glue	glue	glue

Cut out the puzzle.
Glue the pieces in the frame.

Name the Parts

Fill in the blanks.

_ _ _ _

_ _ _

_ _ _ _ _

_ _ _ _

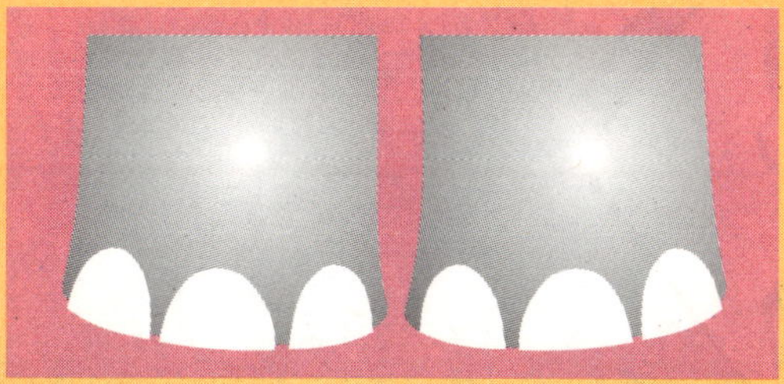

_ _ _ _

_ _ _

Blast Off!

Complete the puzzle. Write the word that names each picture.

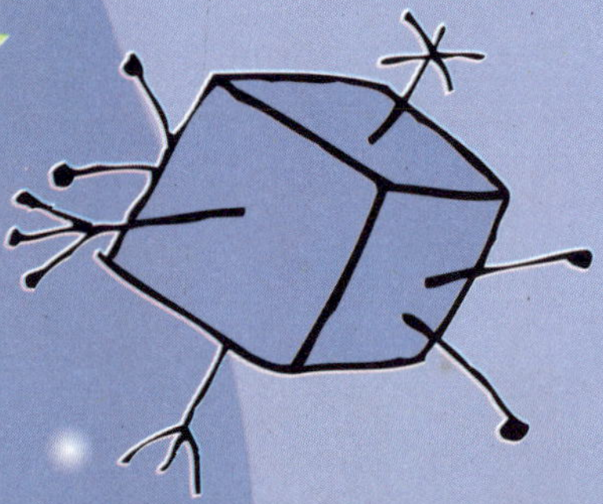

3, 2, 1, blast off!
I leave the Earth behind.
I passed the moon and planets.
I wonder what I'll find?

Who is flying the spaceship?

	s		r		n			t

Word Box

Earth
planet
star
moon
sun

Space Friends

1. Cut out the patterns.
2. Fold on the lines.
3. Glue as shown.
   After the glue dries, put one puppet on each hand.

Let them tell each other about their home planets.

Trouble in Space

List 8 things in this picture that don't make sense.

1 ____________________

2 ____________________

3 ____________________

4 ____________________

5 ____________________

6 ____________________

7 ____________________

8 ____________________

Spacewalk

Connect the dots.

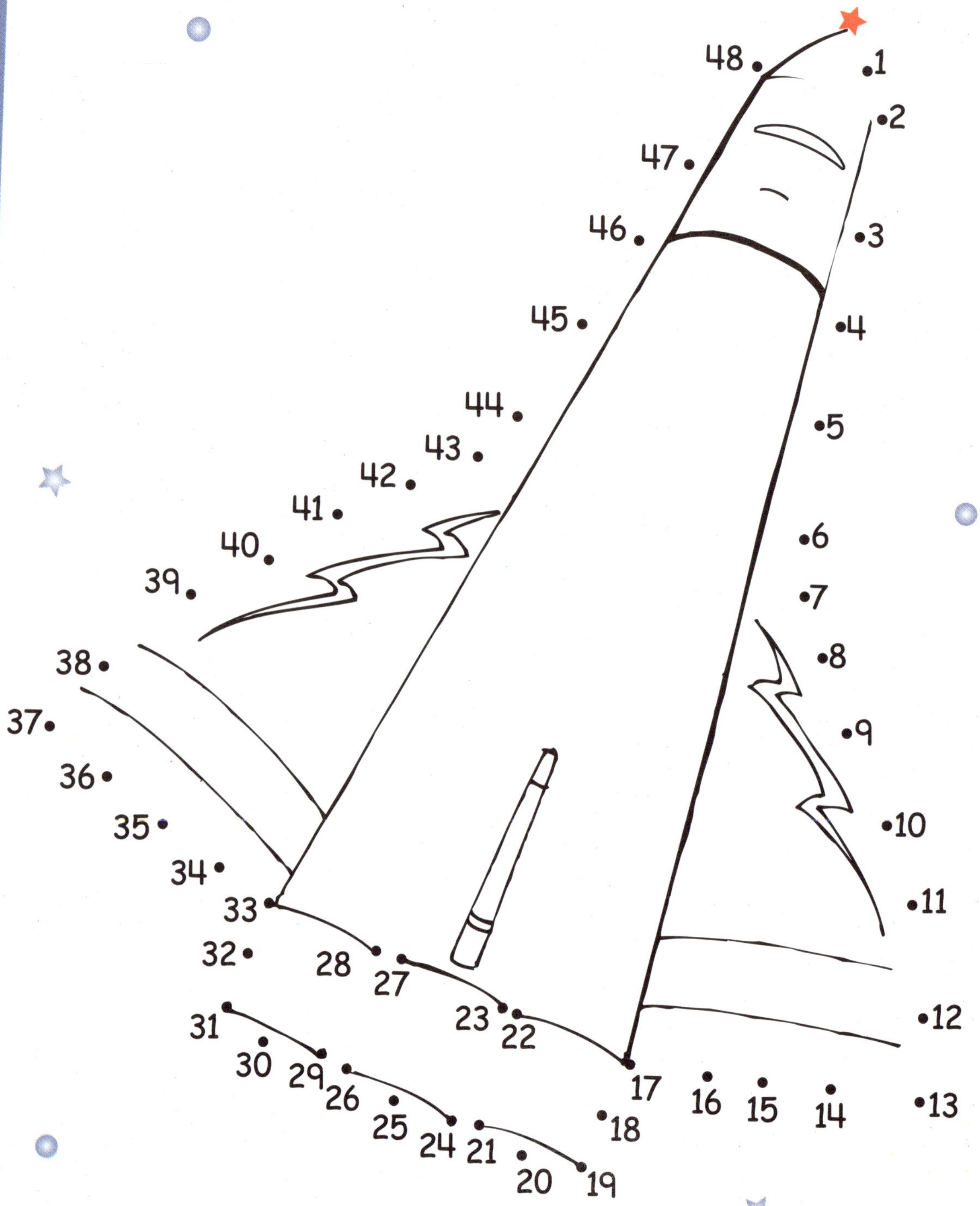

Draw an astronaut on a spacewalk.

Planet X

Help the astronaut find his ship.

Searching Space

Find the words in the puzzle that you see in the word box.

p	l	a	n	e	t	s	s
g	o	m	l	a	s	t	p
u	p	o	a	r	h	a	a
m	r	o	n	t	i	r	c
s	u	n	d	h	p	x	e
b	l	a	s	t	o	f	f

Word Box

	Earth	moon	planet
blast off	star	sun	space

Arms and Legs

Facts

- An octopus has 8 arms called tentacles.
- It lives in the ocean.
- It has a soft body.

Octopus

One arm,
Two arms,
Three arms,
Four!
You mean to say
that you have more?
Five arms,
Six arms,
Seven arms,
Eight!
An octopus is really great!

Leslie Tryon

Facts

- A spider has eight legs.
- It lives on land.
- It has a hard outside cover.

Spider

I saw a spider
start to spin
A spider web
to go hunting in.

Leslie Tryon

Octopus and Spider

How are an octopus and a spider alike?
Make an X if it is true.

	Octopus	Spider
1. I am an animal.		
2. I live in the ocean.		
3. I live on land.		
4. I have 8 legs or 8 arms.		
5. I spin a web.		
6. I have a soft body.		
7. I have a hard outside cover.		
8. I eat other animals.		

My Little Book

Cut out the little book and fold on the lines. Read the story.

Who is squeezed inside this little cave?

An octopus lives here! It has a soft body with no bones. It has little suckers on its arms.

Who has eight legs?
A spider has eight legs.
Who has eight arms?
An octopus has eight arms.

Who spun this web?
A spider spun the web.
The sticky web is used to catch food.

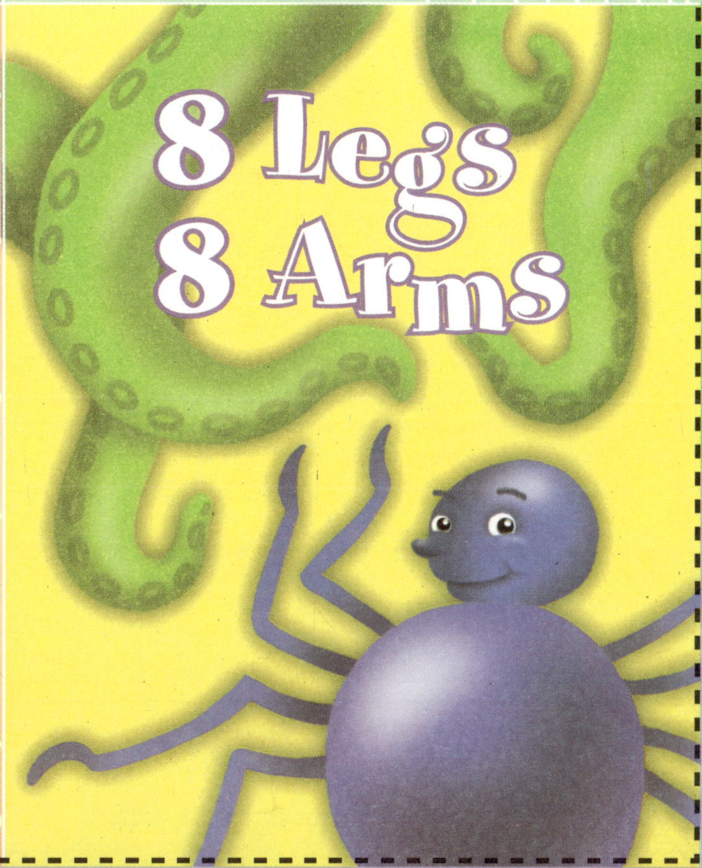

Spiders Everywhere

Circle the three spiders that are alike.

What Am I?

Cut out the pieces.
Glue them in the frame to make a picture.

Octopus Mobile

1. Cut out the octopus patterns on the black dotted lines.
2. Fold down head at tentacles.
3. Cut the tentacles on the white dotted lines.
4. Roll the paper into a tube and glue.
5. Punch holes and use string to tie them to a hanger.

glue
fold
fold

glue
fold
fold

Flying High

Watch the birds fly high.
Watch the birds fly low.
I think it's fun to watch them
Wherever they may go.

I wish I had a pair of wings
And could fly like a bird in the sky.
I'd circle, swoop, and dive
And wave at friends as I flew by.

Jo Ellen Moore

Draw yourself flying in the sky.

Dickey Birds Pop-Up

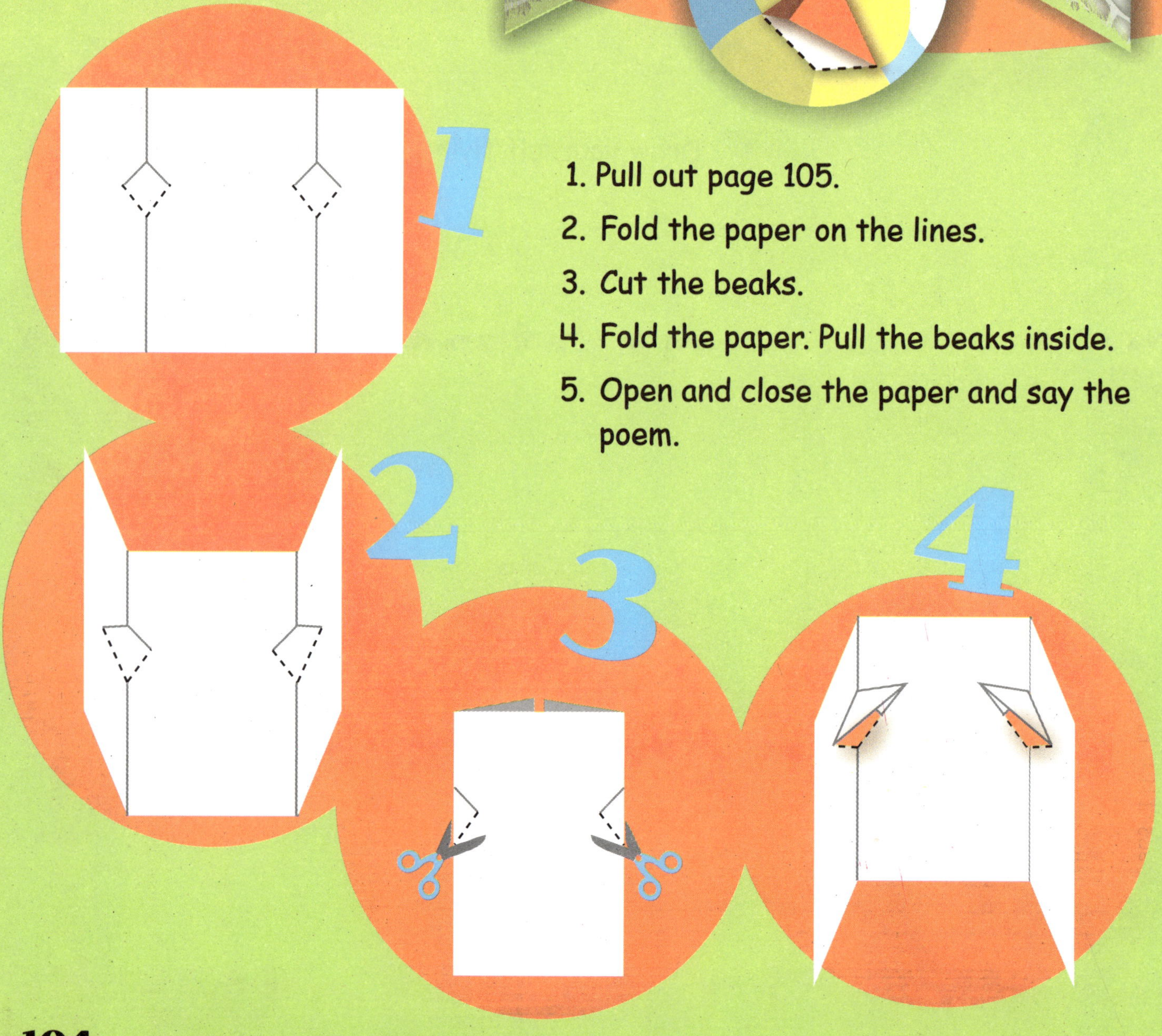

1. Pull out page 105.
2. Fold the paper on the lines.
3. Cut the beaks.
4. Fold the paper. Pull the beaks inside.
5. Open and close the paper and say the poem.

fold
fold
fold
cut
fold
fold
cut
fold
fold
fold
fold
cut
fold
fold
cut

Dickey Birds

Two little dickey birds
Sat on a wall.

One named Peter.
One named Paul.

Fly away, Peter.
Fly away, Paul.

Come back, Peter.
Come back, Paul.

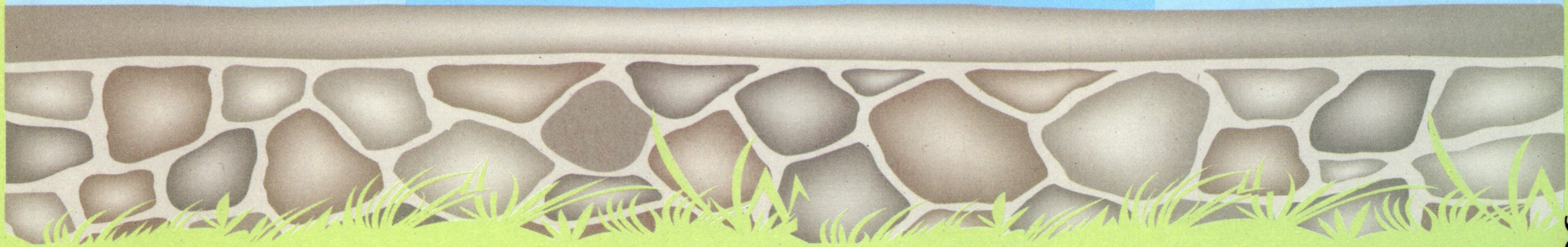

Little Birds in the Nest

Make the birds

1. Cut out the patterns.
2. Fold on the lines.

Make the nest

1. Pull out page 111.
2. Fold on the line.
3. Tape the nest closed on each side. Put the birds in the nest.

Pattern for
Mother Bird

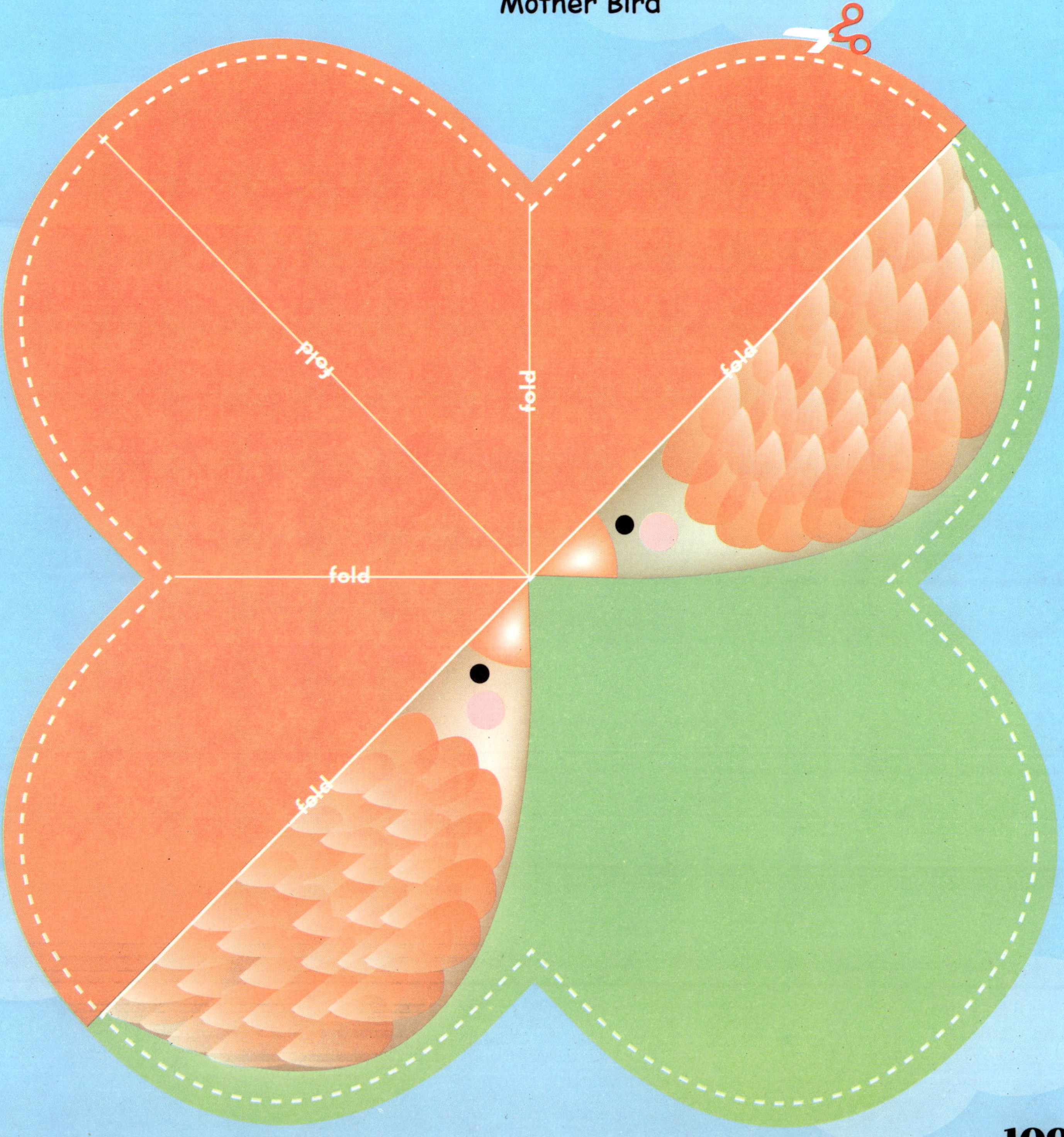

My Bird Nest

fold

glue

glue

Birds of a Feather

Circle the names of birds in the puzzle.

p	p	e	n	g	u	i	n
i	d	r	o	b	i	n	s
g	u	d	r	h	e	n	w
e	c	c	r	o	w	x	a
o	k	l	h	a	w	k	n
n	r	o	o	s	t	e	r

Froggie Fun

Five little speckled frogs
Sitting on a speckled log.
Eating the most delicious flies.
Yum! Yum!

One fell into the pool
Where it was nice and cool.
Now there are four speckled frogs.
Ribbit! Ribbit!

Four little speckled frogs
Sitting on a speckled log.
Eating the most delicious flies.
Yum! Yum!

One fell into the pool
Where it was nice and cool.
Now there are three speckled frogs.
Ribbit! Ribbit!

Three little speckled frogs
Sitting on a speckled log.
Eating the most delicious flies.
Yum! Yum!

One fell into the pool
Where it was nice and cool.
Now there are two speckled frogs.
Ribbit! Ribbit!

Two little speckled frogs
Sitting on a speckled log.
Eating the most delicious flies.
Yum! Yum!

One fell into the pool
Where it was nice and cool.
Now there is one speckled frog.
Ribbit! Ribbit!

Frogs on a Log

1. Cut out the frogs and the log.
2. Accordion-fold the frogs on the lines.
3. Set the frogs on the log.

Frogs

Name the Frogs

Read the clues.
Write the frogs' names on the lines on page 115.

1. Greeny is the last frog.
2. Spot is between Pat and Greeny.
3. Herman is in front of Fred.

Feed the Frog

Make the Frog

1. Cut out the pattern.
2. Fold on the lines.
3. Pull out the pocket. Tape it.
4. Cross the legs. Tape them.

Make the Flies

1. Cut out the patterns.
2. Glue the flies to beans or buttons. Let the glue dry.

Feed the Frog

Toss the flies into the frog's pocket. How far away can you sit and still feed the frog?

fold
fold
fold
fold
fold

A Jungle Frog

Draw the frog and color it.

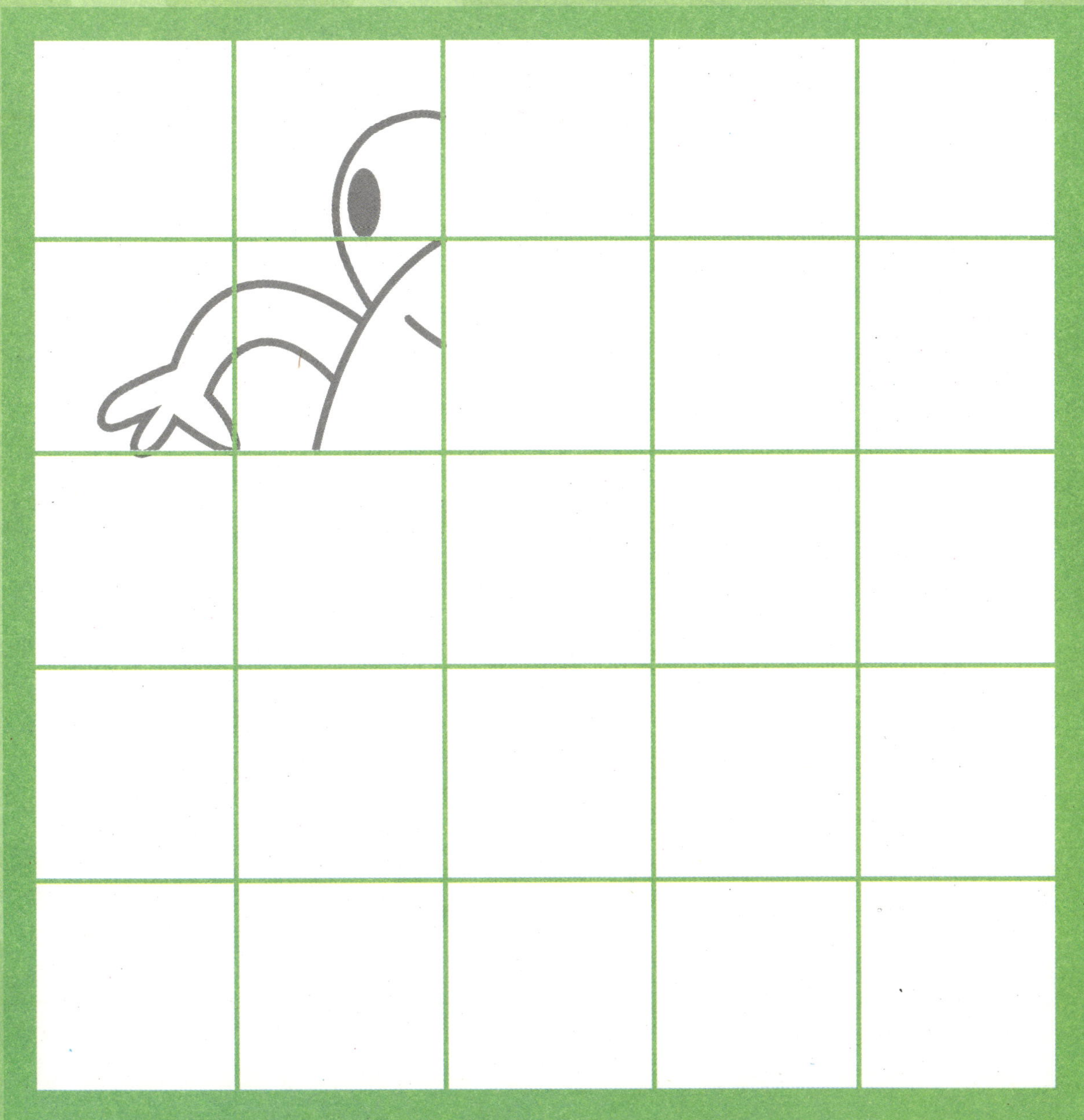

The Tortoise and the Hare

One day, Hare was bragging to the other animals. "None of you is as quick as I am," he said.

Tortoise was passing by. He heard what Hare was saying. "I know who can beat you in a race. I can."

Hare fell down laughing. "How can a poky animal like you beat me?" he said. "I'll race you and I will win!"

The other animals marked a path through the woods. Tortoise and Hare came to the starting line. "Get ready. Get set. Go!" shouted Owl. Off raced Hare as fast as he could go. Soon he was far ahead of Tortoise.

"I think I'll take a little nap under this tree," thought Hare. "Tortoise is so far behind, he will never catch up." Soon Hare was asleep.

Tortoise kept walking. He passed by the sleeping Hare. When Hare woke up from his nap, he couldn't see Tortoise anywhere.

"I knew that silly Tortoise was the slowest animal on Earth," laughed Hare. He started to run again.

Just then Hare heard a shout. "What is that?"

He hurried to the end of the race. He saw that Tortoise was almost to the finish line. The loud shout had been the animals cheering for Tortoise.

Hare raced as fast as he could. It was too late. There was no way he could beat Tortoise. Hare hid his face and crept away.

Tortoise crossed the finish line. His friends shouted, "Hooray for Tortoise!" They patted him on the back.

Hare learned that slow and steady can win the race.

Look Closely

Find one in each row that is different.

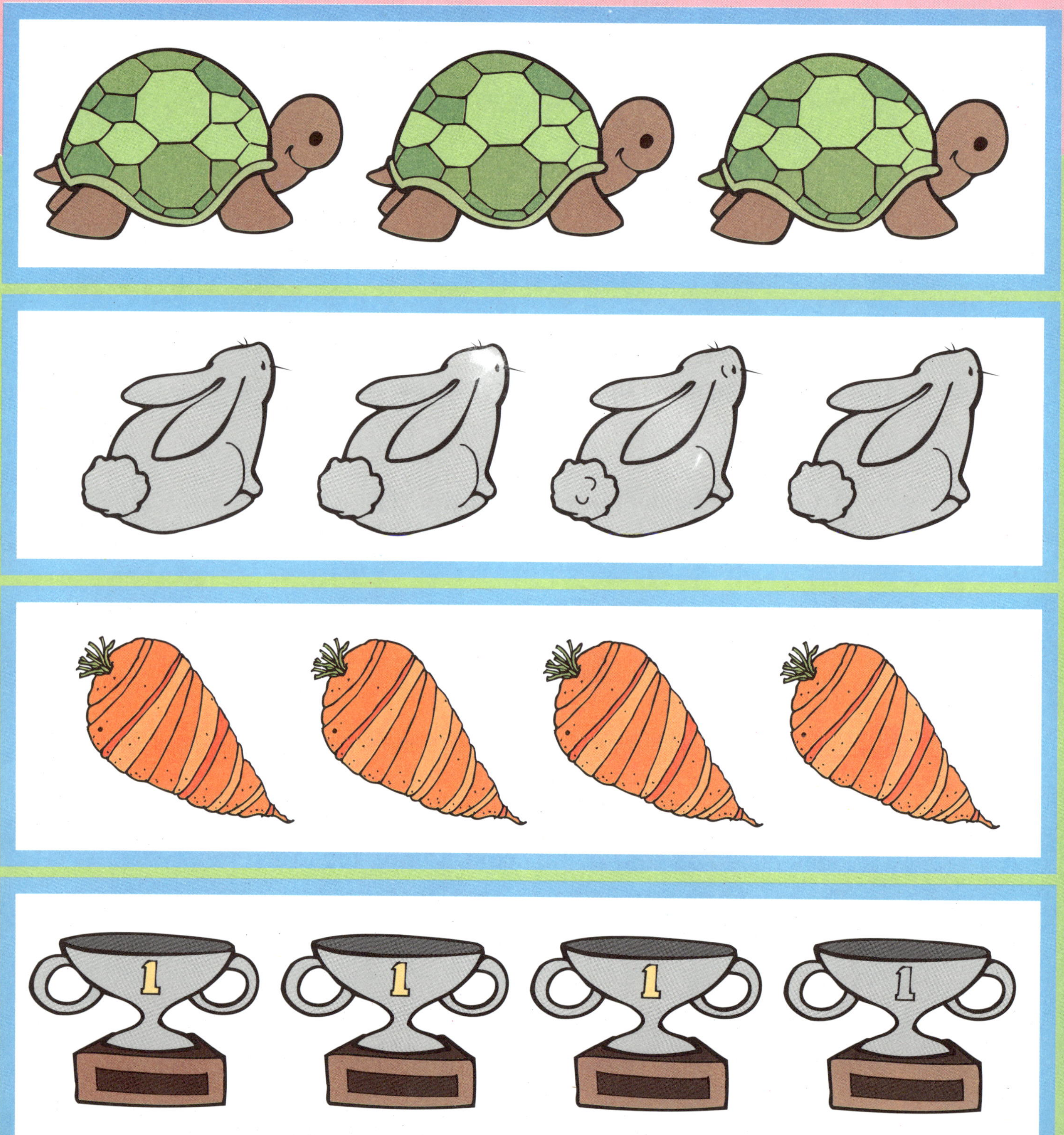

Retell the Story

Cut out the patterns.
Fold on the lines and stand up the characters.
Use the characters to retell the story to a friend.

The Race

Word Box

slow, hare, fast, owl, nap, race, tortoise

Fill in the boxes.

Down

1. tortoise
2. hare
4. not fast
5. sleep

Across

3. not slow
6. owl
7. running contest

The Firehouse

Connect the dots and color.

What Can It Be?

Rrrrr-rrrr-rrrr.
I hear a siren loud and clear.
What can it be?

Rrrrr-rrrr-rrrr.
I see flashing lights coming near.
What can it be?

Rrrrr-rrrr-rrrr.
It's big. It's red. It's stopping here.
What can it be?

It's a fire engine!

Jill Norris

What Is It?

Write the name for each picture.

Word Box

hydrant, ladder, nozzle, hose, helmet, fire extinguisher, hatchet

Brave Helper

glue	glue	glue
glue	glue	glue
glue	glue	glue
glue	glue	glue

Cut out the puzzle pieces.
Glue them on the grid to make a picture.

A Lifesaver

Draw the other side.

At the Fire

Circle what is wrong in the picture on page 135.
Write about the funniest mistake in the picture.

Where's My Mother?

Help Mom find her baby.

Paper Tube Kangaroo

1. Cut out the patterns.
2. Glue the pieces to the back of the paper tube.
3. Tape the baby kangaroo to a pencil or drinking straw. Move it up and down inside the tube to allow it to peek out of Mother's pouch.

Kangaroo Head

Kangaroo Tail

Baby Kangaroo

Kangaroo Body

Baby Animals

Find the animal names. Circle them.

kitten

tadpole

puppy

c	j	o	e	y	d	m
a	c	a	l	f	u	o
t	w	t	r	s	c	k
e	o	a	a	t	k	i
r	l	d	t	i	l	t
p	u	p	p	y	i	t
i	s	o	x	z	n	e
l	m	l	n	x	g	n
l	o	e	f	o	a	l
a	c	h	i	c	k	o
r	f	u	n	n	y	z

joey

caterpillar

chick

duckling

calf

foal

The Chickens

Said the first little chick
With a strange little squirm,
"I wish I could find
A fat little worm."

Said the second little chick
With an odd little shrug,
"I wish I could find
A fat little slug."

Said the third little chick
With a sharp little squeal,
"I wish I could find
Some nice yellow meal."

Said the fourth little chick
With a sigh of grief,
"I wish I could find
A little green leaf."

Said the fifth little chick
With a faint little groan,
"I wish I could find
A wee gravel stone."

"Now, see here," said Mother Hen,
From the green garden patch,
"If you want your breakfast,
Just come here and scratch."

Chicken Chains

1. Cut out the hen and the chick strips.
2. Fold up each strip on the lines.
3. Cut on the black lines.
4. Unfold the strips.
5. Set up the hens and chicks.

Cock-a-Doodle-Doo

Color each rooster differently.

The Mix-Up

Little Red and Big Butter have mixed up their chicks. Help them find their babies.

How many chicks does each hen have?

Little Red ◯ Big Butter ◯

Old MacDonald

Old MacDonald had a farm, ee-ii-ee-ii-oo!
And on that farm he had some ducks, ee-ii-ee-ii-oo!
With a quack, quack here and a quack, quack there,
Here a quack, there a quack, everywhere a quack, quack.
Old MacDonald had a farm, ee-ii-ee-ii-oo!

Old MacDonald had a farm, ee-ii-ee-ii-oo!
And on that farm he had some pigs, ee-ii-ee-ii-oo!
With an oink, oink here and an oink, oink there,
Here an oink, there an oink, everywhere an oink, oink.
Old MacDonald had a farm, ee-ii-ee-ii-oo!

Old MacDonald had a farm, ee-ii-ee-ii-oo!
And on that farm he had some sheep, ee-ii-ee-ii-oo!
With a baa, baa here and a baa, baa there,
Here a baa, there a baa, everywhere a baa, baa.
Old MacDonald had a farm, ee-ii-ee-ii-oo!

Old MacDonald had a farm, ee-ii-ee-ii-oo!
And on that farm he had a horse, ee-ii-ee-ii-oo!
With a neigh, neigh here and a neigh, neigh there,
Here a neigh, there a neigh, everywhere a neigh, neigh.
Old MacDonald had a farm, ee-ii-ee-ii-oo!

In the Barnyard

4

1

2

3

1. Cut out the animals and tree on page 149. Fold on the lines.
2. Cut out the barn on page 151. Cut the lines to make the door. Fold the door open. Fold out the base to glue.
3. Glue the barn on the barnyard sheet as shown.
4. Set up the animals.

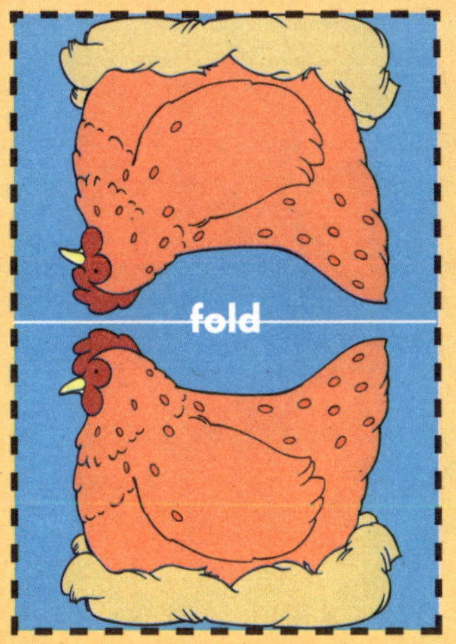
fold

fold

fold

fold

fold

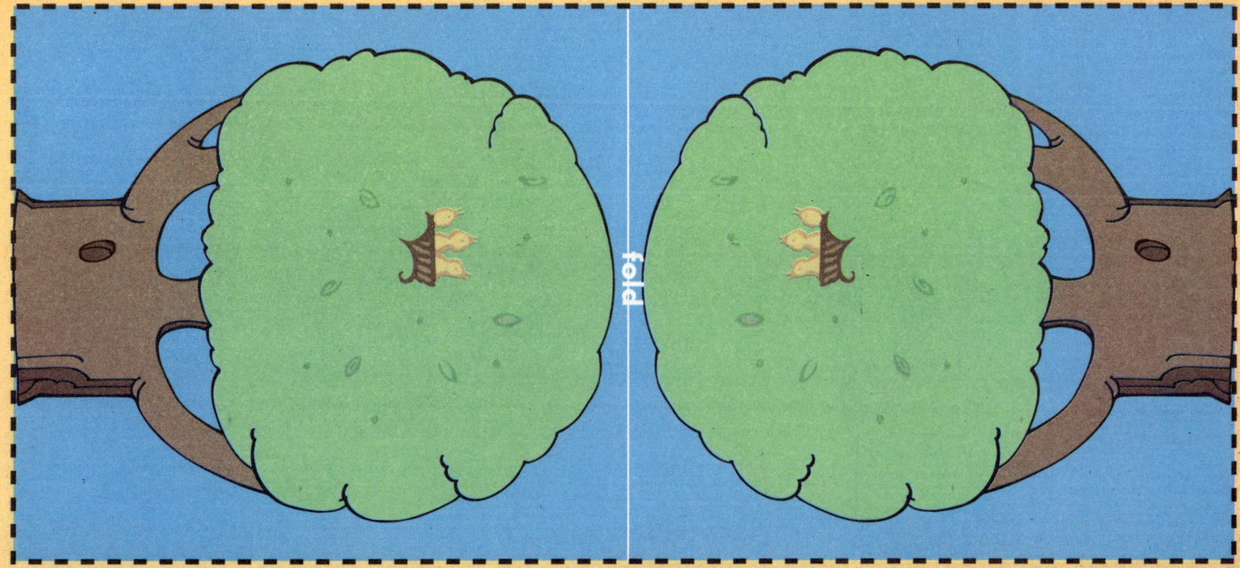
fold

fold
fold
fold
fold
fold

The Barnyard

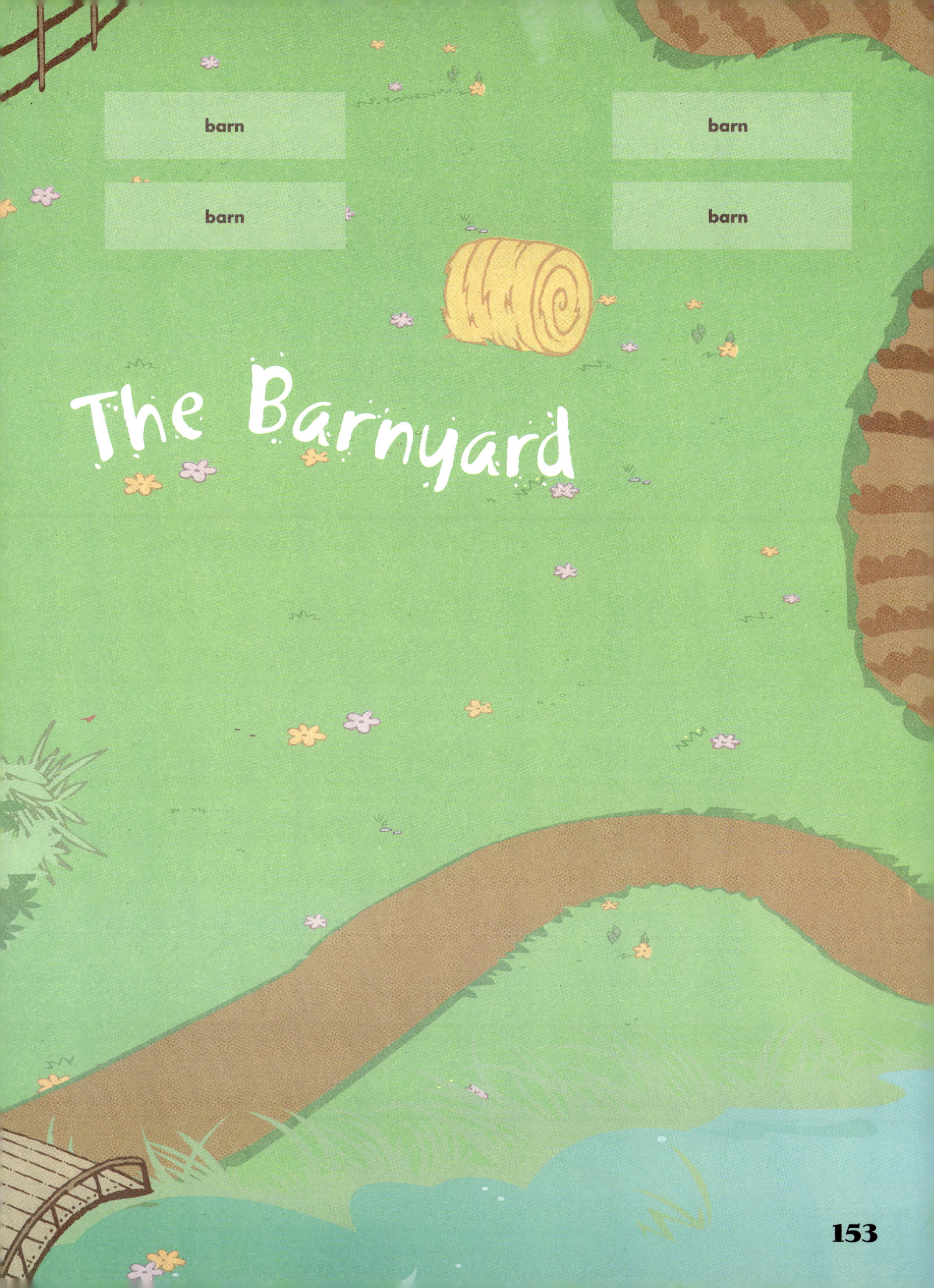

What Sound Do I Make?

Fill in the puzzle.

Answer Key

Page 5

Page 11

Page 12

Page 15

Page 22

Page 23

Page 25

Page 27

Page 28

Page 29

Page 35

Page 36

Page 45

Page 47

Page 51

Page 55

Page 57

Page 65

Page 69

Page 72

Page 73

Page 78

Page 81

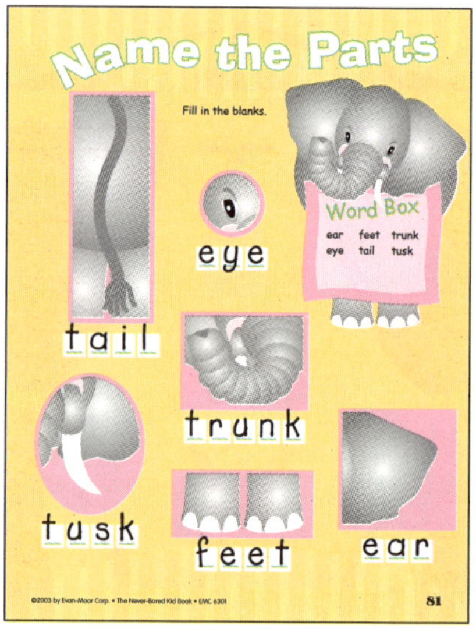

Page 82

Page 83

Page 87

Page 88

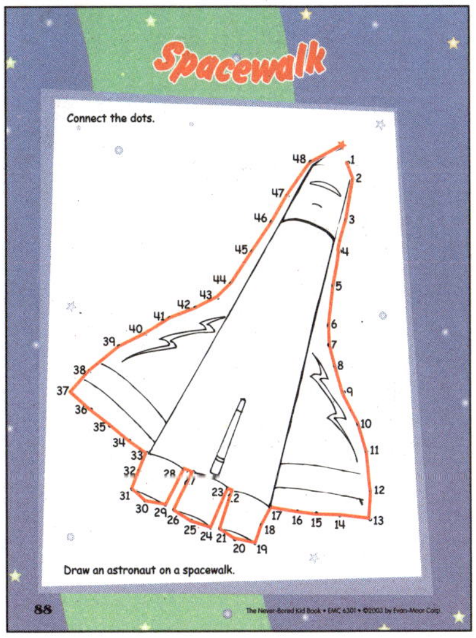

Page 89

Page 90

Page 92

	Octopus	Spider
1. I am an animal.	X	X
2. I live in the ocean.	X	
3. I live on land.		X
4. I have 8 legs or 8 arms.	X	X
5. I spin a web.		X
6. I have a soft body.	X	
7. I have a hard outside cover.		X
8. I eat other animals.	X	X

Page 95

Page 96

Page 113

Page 117

Page 124

Page 127

Page 128

Page 129

Page 130

Page 135

Page 136

Page 141

Page 146

Page 155